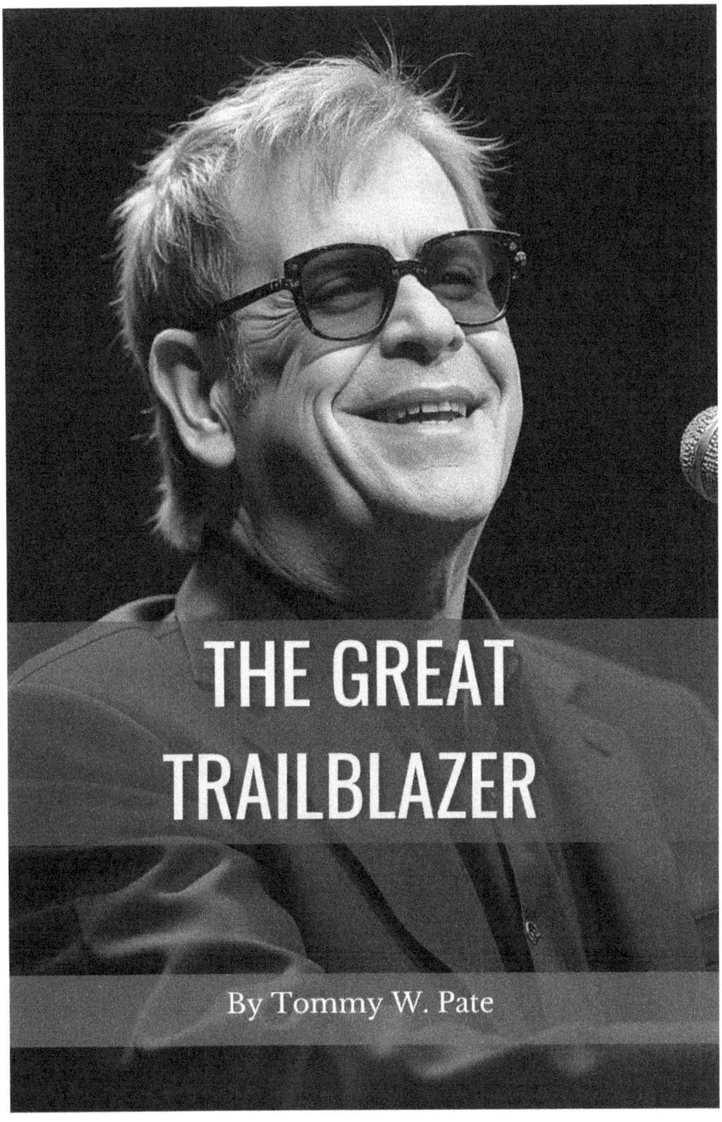

THE GREAT TRAILBLAZER

By Tommy W. Pate

The Great Trailblazer

A Vivid Narrative of the Innovative Ideas, Talents and the Global journey of Elton John as a Musical Legend.

By

Tommy W. Pate

All rights reserved. No part of this publication may be reproduced, distributed, or transmitted in any form or by any means, including photocopying, recording, or other electronic or mechanical methods, without the prior written permission of the publisher, except in the case of brief quotations embodied in critical reviews and certain other noncommercial uses permitted by copyright law.

Copyright © Tommy W. Pate, 2024.

Table of Contents

- Table of Contents...4
- About Me..5
- Preface..6
- **Chapter 1**..10
  - Reginald Dwight..10
  - Discovering the Rocket Man........................17
- **Chapter 2**..26
  - Life in the Spotlight.......................................26
  - Flamboyance and Fame...............................36
- **Chapter 3**..46
  - Philanthropy and Advocacy.........................46
- **Chapter 4**..58
  - Love and Family...58
  - The Later Years – Reinventing the Rocket Man.....69
  - Farewell Yellow Brick Road..........................79
- **Chapter 5**..90
  - Elton's Creative Process..............................90
  - The Man Behind the Legend.......................98
  - Moral and life lessons learned....................100

About Me

Having focused on biographical and narrative writing over four years, dedicated writer Tommy W. Pate is Driven to portray the intricacy of actual events, Pate has a unique ability to transform personal travels into gripping narratives that inspire and teach readers. His work defines deep research, precise attention to detail, and a narrative approach that powerfully brings his subjects to life.

By enabling both well-known persons and individuals to really and insightfully tell their stories throughout his career, Pate has produced biographies appealing to a broad audience. Apart from his expertise in biographies, he is well-known for crafting compelling stories exploring topics of resilience, growth, and human transformation. Pate's commitment to storytelling has won him credibility in his field.

Preface

When I initially began researching Elton John's biography, I was astounded at how much his songs had developed into a soundtrack for much of our lives. His songs are timeless, poignant, and courageous; they not only define the pop culture landscape but also provide millions of people with comfort, joy, and inspiration. As I dug more into his story, I quickly found that the man behind the songs was a fantastic man.

Inspired by Elton John's incredible life full of wins, struggles, and reinventions this book is the outcome of my appreciation for Writing his biography has been a voyage through decades of musical brilliance, personal struggles, and inner growth. Elton's tale is not simply about fame, the music, or the dazzling outfits; it is also about resilience, individualism, and the power of self-expression.

In researching Elton's journey to stardom, his partnerships, his philanthropy, and his advocacy, I attempted to capture what makes him an enduring presence. I approached this project with huge respect for his vast achievements in the world of music and beyond, as well as a real desire to convey the whole tale of the highs, the lows, and everything in between.

I hope this book offers you a deeper insight into the man behind the music, as well as the immense effect he's had on so many lives. Whether you are a lifetime lover or discovering Elton for the first time, may this biography provide insight into his incredible career and the impact he continues to create

Thank you for joining me on this analysis of Elton John's life, a life that has been lived in full color.

Sincerely,   Tommy W. Pate

Introduction

Welcome to the beautiful world of Elton John!

As you open the pages of this book, you're about to embark on a voyage through the life of one of music's most vivid and iconic legends. Elton John's narrative is filled with glittering highs, personal struggles, and unusual encounters that have impacted not only his life but also the world of music as we know it.

Whether you've been a fan for years or you're just discovering the genius behind songs like "Rocket Man" and "Your Song," this biography will take you behind the scenes of his extraordinary career, famous performances, and personal successes. From the unassuming piano prodigy to the international celebrity who altered pop culture, Elton John's life is nothing short of remarkable.

I invite you to sit back, relax, and enjoy this amazing account of a person who, through skill, work, and a lot of heart, built a legend.

Happy reading!

Chapter 1

Reginald Dwight

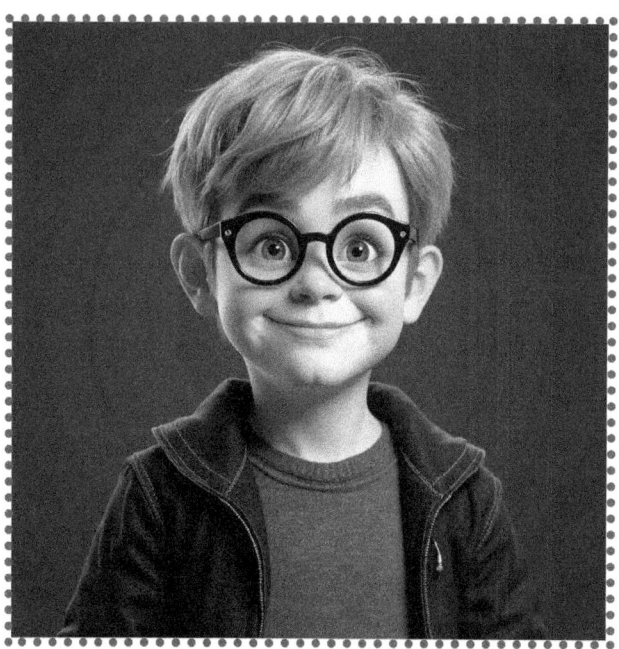

The Early Years

Elton John, born Reginald Kenneth Dwight on March 25, 1947, in Pinner, a little suburban village in Middlesex, England, had humble roots that would one day seem a world away from the extravagant theatrical productions and international reputation he would come to know. His early life was touched by a love of music, family issues, and a sense of longing that would later drive his desire to abandon his surroundings and find sanctuary in the arena of song.

Pinner, at this time, was a pleasant, middle-class suburb, and Reginald's family lived modestly. His parents, Stanley Dwight, a Royal Air Force officer, and Sheila Dwight (née Harris), had a tumultuous relationship that severely influenced the youngster. Stanley was a severe, emotionally disconnected man who disapproved of the music industry, but Sheila, although at times surprising, was a critical source of emotional support and encouragement for Reginald's musical objectives. It was Sheila's love of popular music that first introduced him to the recordings of American rock 'n' roll performers like

Elvis Presley and Bill Haley, which would start a lifelong interest in music.

Reginald's childhood was marked by a sensation of remoteness. His father's frequent absences due to his employment in the Royal Air Force meant that the household was dominated by his mother and his maternal grandmother, Ivy. It was Ivy who played a significant role in establishing Reginald's interest in music. Seeing his burgeoning interest, his parents acquired a secondhand piano when he was just four years old. It was on this instrument that the young kid would first exhibit the musical genius that would later enchant the world.

Reginald's affinity with the piano was immediate. By the age of five, he had begun to teach himself to play by ear, readily picking up songs that he heard on the radio.

His intrinsic ability for the instrument was clear, and soon, he was spending hours at the piano, exploring the keys, and crafting his tunes. It was apparent to anybody who heard him play that this was no normal boy; he had a gift, and the piano became his sanctuary a place where he could escape the constraints of his home life and express himself in ways he couldn't with words Recognizing his outstanding skill, his family enrolled him in formal piano instruction when he was barely seven years old.

Reginald excelled immediately, and after a few years, he obtained a junior scholarship to the famed Royal Academy of Music in London. Attending the academy on weekends, young Reginald excelled in the disciplined setting, and his tutors were astounded by his skill. Despite his lack of professional instruction in reading music at that time, he could recreate complete pieces of classical music after hearing them just once, a feat that surprised his tutors.

While the Royal Academy sharpened his technical talents, Reginald's heart remained with the popular music he heard at home. His enthusiasm for rock 'n' roll continued to develop, and he started to view the piano as a tool not just for classical music but for making his compositions. His admiration for Jerry Lee Lewis, Little Richard, and Ray Charles drove him to explore with diverse approaches, merging classical skills with the energy and thrill of the mainstream music of the day.

However, Reginald's early years were not without suffering. The relationship between his parents continued to deteriorate, and their regular confrontations produced an extremely tumultuous family environment. His father's criticism of Reginald's musical ambitions was a frequent cause of stress. Stanley wanted his son to pursue a more conventional, secure job, and the notion of Reginald being a professional musician sounded absurd to him. This disagreement increased the developing gap between father and son, making the young boy's attachment to the piano even stronger - it became a shelter from the hardships at home.

As a youngster, Reginald was timid, introverted, and frequently found himself feeling out of place. Music became his means of dealing with these emotions of solitude. He took solace in playing, frequently losing himself for hours at the piano, creating a world of sound where he felt secure and in charge. His profound emotional attachment to music, paired with his amazing skill, established the groundwork for what would eventually become a renowned career.

By the time Reginald was a teenager, his passion for music had entirely overtaken him. Though he continued his classical training at the Royal

Academy of Music, he began performing at local pubs and clubs under the stage name "Reg Dwight." These early performances allowed him to develop his stage presence and confidence, even as he struggled with his identity and the expectations placed upon him.

His early experiences with the piano molded the essence of who Elton John would eventually become. From those first moments of discovery as a youngster to his official schooling at the Royal Academy, the piano was not merely an instrument; it was a lifeline. It gave him a form of expression, a way to voice feelings he couldn't describe, and eventually, a road out of the small-town existence that had grown to seem confining.

Though his journey to stardom was just beginning, Reginald Dwight's childhood was the soil from which Elton John would grow a boy whose talent was undeniable, whose love for music was all-consuming, and whose longing for something greater would one day take him beyond Pinner and onto the world stage. The piano, his loyal friend from the very beginning, would stay at the center of his musical journey, as he changed from the shy youngster at the keys into one of the most acclaimed performers in history.

Discovering the Rocket Man

Reginald Kenneth Dwight's metamorphosis into Elton John ranks as one of the most memorable and impactful metamorphoses in the history of popular music. His path from a modest, contemplative young pianist to the flamboyant, larger-than-life rock hero was formed by a complex combination of personal ambition, musical influences, and the cultural zeitgeist of the late 1960s and early 1970s. The invention of the "Elton John" persona signaled the beginning of a career that would see him smash musical limits, revolutionize stage performance, and become a worldwide phenomenon.

From an early age, Reginald's involvement in music was thorough. His classical background at the Royal Academy of Music gave him a solid technical basis, but his heart was with the popular music that dominated the radio and record players of the 1950s and 60s.

Influenced by performers like Elvis Presley, Ray Charles, and Little Richard, young Reginald was intrigued by the intensity and emotional force of rock 'n' roll. These musicians, with their powerful stage presences and ability to connect with audiences via electric performances, provided important influences for the character he would eventually construct.

As a youngster, Reginald started playing in local bands and bar concerts, singing versions of popular songs of the period. In 1962, he co-founded a band called Bluesology, which originally concentrated on performing rhythm & blues.

Though Bluesology experienced small success and acquired a following on the club scene, Reginald found himself longing for a more personal and creative outlet. He felt restricted, both musically and psychologically, by his function in the band and by his identity as Reg Dwight.

His first important move toward metamorphosis occurred in 1967 when he answered an advertisement in the "New Musical Express" issued by Liberty Records, seeking new composers. It was via this that Reginald was introduced to Bernie Taupin, a young lyricist who would become his lifelong partner. Together, they forged one of the most durable and successful songwriting teams in music history.

Taupin would offer the words, sometimes beautiful and complex, while Reginald would construct the melodies and bring the tunes to life. This cooperation provided Reginald the creative freedom he sought, enabling him to explore new musical forms and express himself in ways he hadn't been able to previously.

At this key time, Reginald took the choice to recreate himself fully. Realizing that "Reg Dwight" lacked the star power and charisma he intended to represent, he took the daring step of inventing a new persona. Drawing inspiration from two members of Bluesology—saxophonist **Elton Dean** and vocalist **Long John Baldry**—he adopted the name **"Elton John."** This change marked the beginning of a new chapter in his life, one in which he could shed the limitations of his past and fully embrace his ambitions for stardom.

The name change was more than simply a shift in appellation; it was the birth of a new character. Elton John was not merely a musician he was a performer, an entertainer, and an icon in the making. Alongside his new identity, Elton started to establish a style that would distinguish him apart from his peers.

He liked colorful, dramatic stage outfits, frequently including glitter, feathers, sequins, and huge eyeglasses. These outfits were not only about aesthetics, they were a representation of his larger-than-life personality and his aim to capture people visually as well as musically. Elton John's flamboyant style would go on to define his public image and become one of the most identifiable parts of his career.

What made their cooperation more noticeable was the way their bond evolved alongside their professional one. Although they came from different backgrounds Elton from a working-class London neighborhood and Bernie from rural Lincolnshire the two established a deep and enduring friendship. Their relationship helped them to work past the unavoidable difficulties of fame and creative pressure. Taupin, who was more humble and preferred to keep out of the limelight, gave a calming influence on Elton, whose larger-than-life demeanor and enthusiastic stage presence often grabbed center stage. Together, they survived the highs and lows of the music industry, with Taupin's steadying presence complementing Elton's more volatile public life.

As their careers expanded, the duo continued to enhance their songwriting. In the late 1970s and 1980s, Elton and Bernie experimented with more modern sounds, adding elements of disco, R&B, and electronic music into their work. Songs like "Don't Go Breaking My Heart" and "I'm Still Standing" illustrate the duo's ability to adapt to new musical trends while preserving the essential features of their collaboration—emotionally gripping lyrics and memorable melodies.

In the 1980s, Elton and Bernie briefly separated ways, with Elton engaging with new lyricists for some time. However, they reconnected in the early 1990s, and their partnership once again bloomed. One of the most important occurrences of their later career came in 1997 when Elton re-recorded "Candle in the Wind" as a dedication to Princess Diana following her sad death. The new version, "Candle in the Wind 1997," became one of the best-selling songs of all time, further establishing the pair's place as one of the most successful songwriting duos in history.

Their creative teamwork, although unorthodox, has persisted for more than 50 years, an astounding success in an industry infamous for transient alliances. Throughout their career, Elton and

Bernie have retained an uncompromising regard for each other's abilities. While Elton's musical skill brought the lyrics to life, he has always credited Taupin for delivering the words that established the emotional basis of their tunes. Conversely, Taupin has always claimed praise for Elton's ability to transform his thoughts into music that resonates with audiences worldwide.

The foundation of their partnership lies in the optimal balance of Taupin's lyrical story and Elton's musical sensibilities. Together, they have developed a body of work that spans genres and decades, delivering songs that are not only monetarily successful but also deeply essential to millions of listeners. From the contemplative beauty of "Your Song" to the anthemic intensity of "Rocket Man" and "Goodbye Yellow Brick Road," their songs have survived the test of time, continuing to inspire new generations of admirers.

In the end, the bond between Elton John and Bernie Taupin is more than merely a musical partnership; it is a monument to the power of creative synergy and mutual respect. Their melodies have become an indelible part of the cultural fabric, and their impact on present music is apparent. Even after five decades, their music remains as contemporary and fascinating as ever, and their place as one of the greatest songwriting duos in history is firmly entrenched.

Chapter 2

Life in the Spotlight

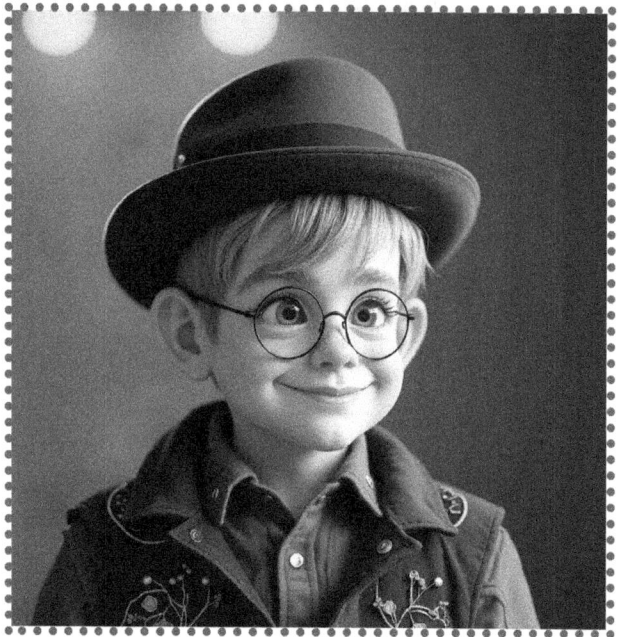

Navigating celebrity, excess, and the pressures of being one of the world's top pop musicians is a tough and usually traumatic journey, one that Elton John experienced firsthand in the whirlwind of his climb to international prominence.

Elton's journey to fame was as rapid as it was terrifying, and the stresses of living under continual public scrutiny, mixed with the temptations and indulgences of rock 'n' roll excess, took a great toll on his personal life. Yet, despite the ups and downs, Elton managed to survive, ultimately emerging stronger and more self-aware.

Elton John's stunning ascension began in the early 1970s, and by the middle of the decade, he was one of the finest performers in the world. His dramatic stage look, together with his immense abilities as a pianist and writer, soon made him an international sensation.

Hits like "Rocket Man," "Goodbye Yellow Brick Road," and "Crocodile Rock" dominated the charts, and his albums sold millions of copies worldwide. However, fame and success came with a price: the loss of isolation, the pressure to continually deliver hits, and the severe demands of a rigorous touring schedule.

As Elton's celebrity expanded, so did the expectations placed upon him. In the public eye, he was larger than life, usually seen in lavish attire and acting with a degree of passion that appeared superhuman.

His performance style was dazzling feathers, sequins, platform boots, and flashy sunglasses were his trademarks, and audiences couldn't get enough. But behind the scenes, Elton was attempting to preserve a sense of balance in a culture that was quickly spiraling out of control.

One of the greatest problems Elton faced during this period was the obligation to live up to the image he had constructed. The Elton John that audiences liked was brave, adventurous, and attractive, but the actual Elton Reginald Dwight was significantly more frail.

As someone who had grown up shy and introverted, Elton often found it difficult to reconcile the two elements of himself. The more his notoriety climbed, the more he felt the need to keep up appearances, even while the strains of success were taking a toll on his mental health.

The 1970s was also an age of immense luxury in the music industry, and Elton was not immune to the temptations that came with celebrity. The lifestyle of a rock star, especially one as successful as Elton, was marked by a hedonistic mix of sex, drugs, and non stop partying. As his notoriety soared, Elton found himself increasingly seduced into the trappings of celebrity life, dabbling in drink and drugs to cope with the stress of fame and the demands of continual touring.

Cocaine, in particular, constituted a crucial element of Elton's life during this era. What began as a tactic to better his performances and preserve his high-energy stage persona eventually turned into an addiction that had serious repercussions for his health and well-being.

The drug allowed him to remain up for days on end, pushing himself beyond normal limitations, but it also led to erratic behavior, mental instability, and physical tiredness. Behind the scenes, Elton was trying to keep himself together, even as he continued to provide spectacular performances week after night.

The demands of stardom frequently lead to personal isolation. Although Elton was usually surrounded by people managers, assistants, musicians, and fans he often felt incredibly lonely. The incessant traveling, the never-ending cycle of recording and marketing, and the lack of a real home life left him feeling distant from the people closest to him. His relationships worsened as a result, and despite his public image as a fun-loving, flamboyant performer, Elton grappled with sentiments of despair and self-doubt.

In addition to the emotional load of popularity, Elton also endured the physical toll of his unyielding work schedule. By the mid-1970s, he was one of the hardest-working musicians in the industry, playing over 100 performances a year, usually in numerous cities and countries, with little time for vacation in between. The rigorous pace of life on the road left him physically fatigued, but the need to keep delivering hit after strike meant there was little time for recuperation. The responsibilities of preserving his career trajectory were considerable, and the persistent desire to stay at the top of the charts added to the stress.

Elton's fight with his identity and sexuality further heightened the stresses of popularity. In the 1970s, homosexuality was still exceedingly taboo, and although Elton had relationships with both men and women, he kept his genuine sexual orientation concealed for much of his early career.

In 1976, he officially came out as bisexual in an interview with "Rolling Stone", a brave step at the time, but it wasn't until many years later that he completely accepted his identity as a homosexual man. This internal conflict, along with the external demands of being a public person, generated a feeling of inner turmoil that contributed to his drug usage and mental instability.

The late 1970s and early 1980s were exceedingly tough for Elton. Although his career survived, he got more hooked on drugs and alcohol to cope with the pressures of notoriety. His behavior got more erratic, and he constantly found himself in confrontations with people around him, especially his long standing lyricist and creative partner Bernie Taupin. The two momentarily broke up in the late 1970s, a reflection of the strain that Elton's issues were placing on his business contacts. During this era, Elton also began to face serious health challenges, including episodes of exhaustion and illness, as a result of his expensive lifestyle.

By the mid-1980s, Elton recognized that he was headed down a risky path. His drug addiction, mental instability, and physical decline had reached a breaking point. After years of denial, Elton ultimately sought treatment, entering rehabilitation in 1990 to face his addiction and begin the journey of recovery. This decision was a turning moment in his life, both emotionally and professionally. For the first time in years, Elton decided to face the issues that had dogged him throughout his career and made moves to take control of his life.

Elton's recovery was not just about beating addiction; it was also about restoring a sense of balance and purpose outside of the cyclone of notoriety. He began to focus more on his health, both physical and mental, and worked to mend the relationships that had been ruined by his years of excess. His bond with Bernie Taupin was renewed, and together they continued to compose music that resonated with audiences throughout the world.

One of the most crucial components of Elton's post-recovery life has been his dedication to charity and advocacy. In 1992, he created the Elton John AIDS Foundation, which has now become one of the world's leading organizations in the struggle against HIV/AIDS. Elton's passion for this cause, spurred by the loss of many friends to the disease, has become a major part of his legacy, and his foundation has generated hundreds of millions of dollars for HIV/AIDS prevention and treatment projects.

As Elton entered the concluding years of his career, he found a new level of happiness, both in his music and in his personal life. His 1993 meeting with David Furnish, who would later become his spouse, marked the beginning of a strong and loving partnership that afforded Elton the support and companionship he had long sought. In 2010, the couple welcomed their first child, Zachary, followed by a second son, Elijah, in 2013. Fatherhood brought Elton a huge sense of satisfaction and purpose, grounding him in ways that stardom and fortune never could.

Despite the immense difficulties he experienced over his career, Elton John's ability to handle fame, excess, and the strains of living as a global superstar is a tribute to his persistence and ambition. His trek from addiction and personal conflict to sobriety and stability is not just a dramatic story of redemption but also a reminder of the human toll that stardom can take on even the most successful and resilient folks. Today, Elton John stands not only as one of the greatest performers of all time but also as a symbol of fortitude, survival, and the power of reinvention.

Flamboyance and Fame

Elton John's extravagant outfit choices, dazzling stage performances, and larger-than-life personality not only transformed what it meant to be a pop star but also revolutionized the expectations of what a live concert could be. From the early days of his career, Elton blended costumes and performance to reflect his persona, delivering a visual and musical spectacular that thrilled audiences throughout the world. His lavish attire, strange accessories, and exuberant performances were as famous as his music, making him one of the most known and influential figures in popular culture.

When Elton originally began his career in the late 1960s, he appeared pretty modest compared to the flashy figure he would later establish. In the early days, he dressed modestly, typically in slacks and plain shirts. However, as his confidence soared and his reputation surged, Elton began experimenting with his look, developing a style that mirrored the quirky and brilliance of his songs. By the 1970s, he had thoroughly embraced his love for the theatrical, and his performances were immersive experiences, mixing music, costumes, and performance art in ways that had never been seen before in popular music.

One of the most apparent elements of Elton John's wardrobe progression was his propensity for wearing lavish clothes that strained the confines of typical pop star apparel. Rather than complying to the conventional rock star uniform of leather jackets and trousers, Elton opted for colorful, often extravagant attire that ranged from rhinestone-covered jumpsuits to feathered capes and giant platform boots.

His outfit choices were not merely a form of self-expression but also a tool to challenge the ideals of gender and identity in the music industry. He routinely blurred the lines between masculine and feminine fashion, donning clothes that incorporated sequins, feathers, and fur, characteristics generally associated with women's fashion.

In the 1970s, Elton's costume got even more opulent under the influence of designer Bob Mackie, who was famous for his work with Cher and other celebrities. Mackie's designs for Elton were over-the-top, featuring a range of feathers, diamonds, and daring forms.

One of his most legendary costumes was a glittering Dodger Stadium uniform that Elton sported for his 1975 performance at Dodger Stadium in Los Angeles. The glittery baseball outfit, complete with a matching helmet, demonstrated Elton's ability to merge his love of spectacle with humor and creativity.

This concert, attended by approximately 100,000 people, is one of the most legendary performances in rock history, mainly because of the visual impact of his attire and stage presence.

Elton's penchant for spectacles had become a defining component of his persona. Throughout his career, he has sported a range of crazy, huge spectacles in every form, color, and style possible. From star-shaped frames to glasses encrusted with diamonds, Elton's eyewear was a significant component of his fashion image. His glasses were connected with his appearance, symbolizing his hilarious, uninhibited approach to both his music and his style. For Elton, clothing was not only about aesthetics—it was a tool to enhance his presence and engage his audience on a visceral level.

Elton's stunning theatrical performances went hand in hand with his clothing selections. His performances were legendary for their passion, creativity, and theatricality. He didn't merely play the piano; he embraced the music, often leaping on top of the instrument, dancing across the stage, and connecting with the audience in a way that made every performance feel like a personal meeting. His performances were a blend of high-energy rock 'n' roll and Broadway-style theatrics, with each show involving finely made costumes and stage décor that complimented the story of his songs.

Throughout the 1970s and 1980s, Elton's theatrical presentations became even more elaborate, generally featuring gigantic props, complex lighting, and special effects. He wasn't content with merely singing and playing the piano—he wanted to produce a performance. For example, during his performances of "Bennie and the Jets,"

Elton would sometimes play on a piano that was fitted with lights that flashed in tempo with the song, letting the piano itself become part of the visual spectacle. In this technique, Elton dissolved the lines between musician and performer, pushing the performance experience to new heights of exhilaration.

In many aspects, Elton's style of performance was influenced by the glam rock movement of the 1970s, which promoted androgyny, theatricality, and the defiance of established gender standards. Artists like David Bowie and Marc Bolan were contemporaries who also liked this blending of design and performance, but Elton pushed it to another level with his over-the-top costumes and the vast magnitude of his shows. While many of his friends used fashion to make statements about identity or rebellion, Elton embraced it as a weapon of celebration—of originality, inventiveness, and freedom.

Elton's audacity extended beyond his on-stage character; he was also a pioneer in redefining what it meant to be a pop star in terms of public image and personal identity. At a moment when the music industry was still very much a boys' club, governed by macho rock artists, Elton's flamboyant flair and candor about his sexuality upset the status quo. His inability to conform to normal conceptions of masculinity made him a trailblazer for later generations of artists who desired to express their actual selves without fear of censure.

Elton's impact on attire and performance has been significant and consistent. Many singers who came after him, from Madonna to Lady Gaga, have recognized him as a crucial influence in their approach to mixing music, design, and spectacle. His boldness in expressing his individuality via clothing opened the door for other artists to develop their creativity in ways that went beyond music, helping to rethink the status of the pop star as not merely a musician but a cultural icon.

Beyond the sphere of music, Elton's clothing style has had a great impact on the fashion sector itself. Designers like Gianni Versace, Donatella Versace, and Gucci's Alessandro Michele have all drawn inspiration from Elton's famed looks, leveraging his influence to inspire their creations. Elton's fascination with fashion stays strong to this day—his work with Gucci in the 2010s resulted in a collection of garments that paid homage to some of his most memorable outfits from the 1970s and 1980s. This continuous association between Elton and the fashion industry shows the lasting relevance of his flamboyant style choices.

Ultimately, Elton John's clothes and stage performances were not simply about spectacle—they were about expressing his individuality and breaking down limits. He refused to be pigeonholed or restricted by cultural conventions, and his unapologetic acceptance of his personality helped pave the way for a more inclusive and creative approach to both music and performance. In doing so, he changed what it meant to be a pop star, showing the world that tremendous originality comes not just from the song itself but from the entirety of one's expression—fashion, performance, and personal identity all working together to produce something unforgettable.

Elton John's audacious choices—both in dress and in his performances—set a new threshold for pop stardom. He changed the concert stage into a realm of fantasy, where music, costumes, and theatricality blended into one experience. By stretching the borders of what a pop star may be, Elton not only solidified his spot in music history but also created a lasting impression on the culture at large, indicating that the most memorable stars are those who dare to be different.

Chapter 3

Philanthropy and Advocacy

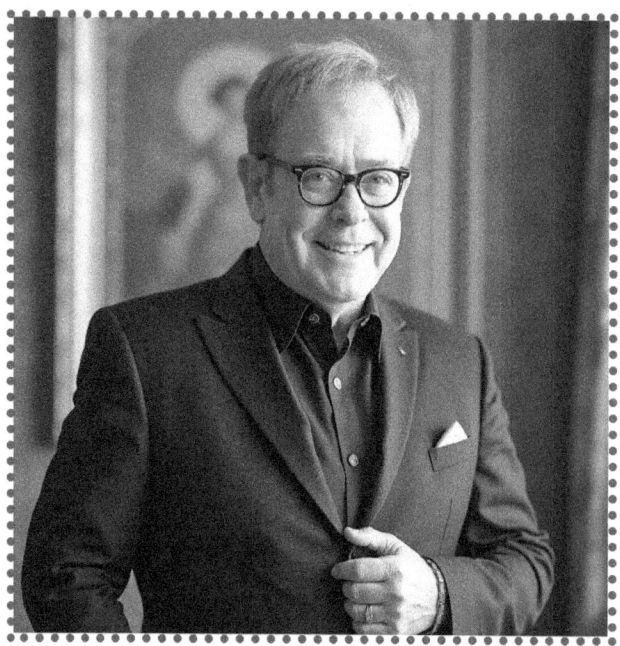

Elton John's involvement in the battle against HIV/AIDS and his support for LGBTQ+ rights is a vital and defining component of his legacy. Over the decades, his efforts have surpassed his musical triumphs, turning him into one of the most important benefactors and champions in global health and the LGBTQ+ movement. Through the foundation of the Elton John AIDS Foundation (EJAF) and his persistent efforts to promote awareness, support research, and fight stigma, Elton has become a driving force in the struggle against one of the most terrible diseases of our time.

The Impact of HIV/AIDS on Elton's Life
The AIDS epidemic of the 1980s greatly impacted Elton John, not only because it destroyed the LGBTQ+ community, of which he was a member, but also because it took the lives of many of his close friends. At the height of the pandemic, the illness carried a severe stigma, especially toward homosexual men, and was frequently treated with fear, disinformation, and widespread apathy from governments and society. In the early years, Elton watched as friends, colleagues, and other artists succumbed to the sickness, unable to halt the havoc

it was doing on people he cared about. This personal tragedy, along with the lack of support for HIV/AIDS patients, spurred his drive to make a difference.

At this time, Elton was battling with his difficulties, including addiction, despair, and the hurdles of managing stardom. As a consequence, he wasn't yet in a situation to take immediate action. However, after entering therapy in 1990 and staying clean, Elton felt forced to channel his energies into making a significant effect. His newfound insight, along with the pain he felt from losing so many loved ones to AIDS, gave him the motivation to become a prominent and energetic supporter in the battle against the illness.

Founding the Elton John AIDS Foundation (EJAF)

In 1992, Elton John launched the Elton John AIDS Foundation (EJAF) as a strategy to confront the HIV/AIDS issue head-on. His objective was modest but ambitious: to limit the spread of HIV, offer care and treatment for people living with the infection, and eventually halt the AIDS pandemic. With a personal wealth and worldwide platform at his disposal, Elton aspired to leverage his resources and influence to achieve genuine change in the battle against HIV/AIDS.

From its founding, the foundation focused on sponsoring initiatives that benefited underserved and at-risk populations, including homosexual men, transgender persons, sex workers, and people of color, all of whom were disproportionately impacted by the pandemic. EJAF aims not only to offer crucial funds for HIV/AIDS treatment and preventive initiatives but also to battle the stigma and prejudice suffered by persons living with the illness.

One of EJAF's early focuses was to finance grassroots groups and community-based initiatives that were already working on the front lines of the epidemic. These groups generally lacked the means or awareness to have a wider impact, but via Elton's foundation, they were able to extend their reach and effectiveness. Over the years, EJAF has granted funding to hundreds of groups across the globe, supporting everything from HIV testing and treatment to education and advocacy campaigns.

Breaking Down Stigma and Raising Awareness

A crucial component of Elton's work in the battle against HIV/AIDS has been his attempts to break down the stigma surrounding the illness. In the early years of the pandemic, HIV/AIDS was widely seen as a "gay disease," and people affected were routinely shunned or stigmatized. This stigma not only made it difficult for individuals to seek care but also fostered misinformation and fear, which in turn encouraged the spread of the virus. Elton utilized his position to fight these detrimental assumptions, speaking frankly about the facts of the pandemic and appealing for more compassion and understanding.

In public remarks, interviews, and even at his performances, Elton utilized his prominence to campaign for individuals impacted by HIV/AIDS, stressing that the illness was not restricted to any one group and that everyone, regardless of sexual orientation, race, or origin, might be affected. His stature as a worldwide icon helped attract attention to the disease in ways that conventional lobbying typically could not. Through his notoriety, Elton was able to reach audiences who may not otherwise have paid attention to the situation, helping to educate and motivate individuals from all walks of life.

Beyond awareness, Elton also attempted to influence public policy. He has long been a prominent critic of governments and organizations that have failed to appropriately handle the AIDS issue, especially in places where political or cultural constraints impede effective action. In 2014, for example, Elton came out against Russia's discriminatory legislation targeting LGBTQ+ persons, stating that such regulations impeded efforts to eradicate HIV/AIDS in the nation. By utilizing his position to point out these abuses, Elton has helped to hold governments responsible and work for policies that prioritize public health and human rights.

Expanding Global Reach and Influence

Under Elton's guidance, EJAF extended its work to a worldwide scale, with offices in both the United States and the United Kingdom. The organization has raised over $600 million since its founding, making it one of the biggest and most successful AIDS charities in the world. Through cooperation with other charitable organizations, governments, and international agencies, EJAF has sponsored projects in more than 55 countries, especially in locations where HIV/AIDS remains a serious public health concern, such as sub-Saharan Africa and Southeast Asia.

Elton has also played a vital role in motivating other high-profile persons to join the battle against HIV/AIDS. He has worked closely with other celebrities, legislators, and business leaders to raise cash and awareness, staging yearly fundraising galas and events that have brought in millions of dollars for the cause. His annual Academy Awards Viewing Party, for example, has become one of the most high-profile fundraising events in Hollywood, earning millions each year to help HIV/AIDS charities.

Advocacy for LGBTQ+ Rights

Elton John's efforts in the battle against HIV/AIDS have always been strongly related to his campaign for LGBTQ+ rights. As a homosexual man who came out publicly in 1976 and subsequently married his long-term boyfriend, David Furnish, Elton has been a prominent presence in the LGBTQ+ community for decades. His personal experiences of growing up during a period when homosexuality was stigmatized, combined with the terrible losses he observed during the AIDS pandemic, made him intensely aware of the prejudice and marginalization encountered by LGBTQ+ persons.

Throughout his career, Elton has been an ardent champion for LGBTQ+ rights, both in the context of HIV/AIDS and more generally. He has continually utilized his position to fight for more acceptance, equality, and protection for LGBTQ+ individuals, whether it is by contesting discriminatory laws, supporting marriage equality, or campaigning for transgender rights. His efforts have not only served to raise awareness of the challenges affecting the LGBTQ+ community but also offered much-needed exposure and recognition for people who often felt invisible or unheard.

Elton's marriage to David Furnish in 2014, following the legalization of same-sex marriage in the UK, was a dramatic statement in favor of LGBTQ+ rights. The pair had been one among the first to join into a civil partnership when the UK legalized them in 2005, and their marriage was viewed as a success for equality. Elton has subsequently continued to work for LGBTQ+ rights across the globe, especially in countries where homosexuality remains criminalized or where LGBTQ+ persons endure violence and persecution.

A Lasting Legacy

Elton John's efforts in the battle against HIV/AIDS and his support for LGBTQ+ rights has left an everlasting effect on both causes. Through EJAF, he has helped to finance essential research, offer life-saving treatment, and support advocacy initiatives that have improved the lives of millions of people throughout the globe. His efforts to promote awareness and battle stigma have revolutionized public attitudes of HIV/AIDS, and his passion for LGBTQ+ equality has inspired many others to continue the struggle for human rights.

What makes Elton's efforts even more noteworthy is the human passion and devotion behind them. This is not only a cause that he supports from a distance; it is a very personal purpose created out of his own experiences, losses, and successes. Elton's advocacy has always been motivated by a tremendous sense of duty to utilize his celebrity and money for the greater good, and he has continuously proved that he is prepared to spend his passion, time, and resources into making the world a better place.

Today, Elton John remains one of the most important voices in the battle against HIV/AIDS and a proponent of LGBTQ+ rights. His charity continues to lead the fight to eliminate the pandemic, while his advocacy work acts as a light of hope and resilience for underprivileged populations globally.

Chapter 4

Love and Family

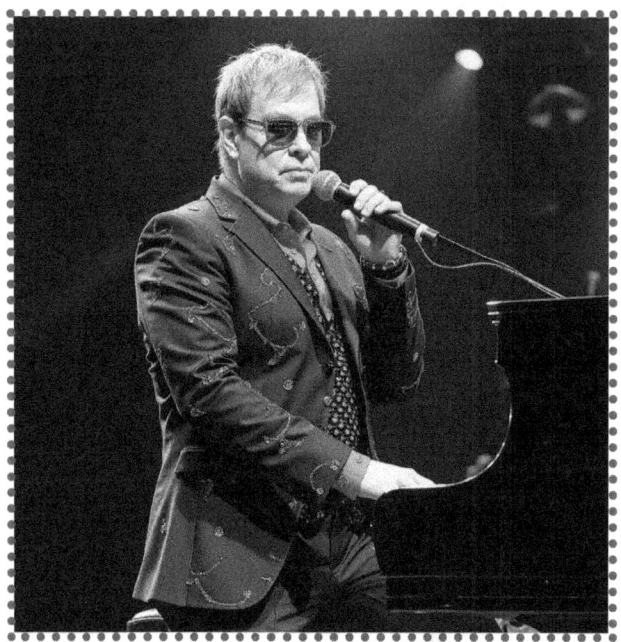

Elton John's connections, notably his marriage to **David Furnish** and his path into parenthood, represent one of the most joyful and rewarding portions of his life narrative. After negotiating years of emotional upheaval, public scrutiny, and inner struggle, Elton discovered stability and great satisfaction in his relationship with Furnish and the thrill of being a parent. Their narrative not only displays Elton's progress but also demonstrates his commitment to living a genuine, loving life despite the hurdles he experienced along the way.

Early Struggles with Love and Identity

Before meeting David Furnish, Elton John's relationships were distinguished by a confusing combination of secret, struggle, and public conjecture. For much of his early career, Elton grappled with his sexual identity while maintaining a public image that was mainly influenced by cultural expectations. In the 1970s, at the zenith of his success, he came out as bisexual in an interview with "Rolling Stone", which was a big step for the time, but it didn't completely represent his actual nature.

In 1984, Elton went into a marriage with Renate Blauel, a German sound engineer, in what many feel was an effort to adapt to a more normal lifestyle or to shelter himself from the rising concerns surrounding his personal life.

The marriage was short-lived, lasting barely four years, and it was apparent that Elton was still battling to embrace his sexuality and live truly. The emotional aftermath from this era, along with his fight with addiction, left him feeling estranged from himself and others. It wasn't until the late 1980s, when Elton began his road to recovery, that he started to come to grips with his actual personality and reconstruct his personal life.

Meeting David Furnish: A Turning Point
Elton's life took a dramatic and positive change when he met David Furnish in 1993. At the time, Furnish, a Canadian-born advertising executive filmmaker, was residing in London. Unlike many

of Elton's prior relationships, which were frequently formed by the turbulent world of celebrity and drug misuse, his bond with Furnish was anchored in stability, mutual respect, and true love. The two met during a dinner party that Elton organized, and their connection evolved swiftly. Furnish's calm and down-to-earth temperament was the ideal counterpoint to Elton's more flashy and fast-paced existence.

For Elton, this connection was different. By the time he met David, Elton had been sober for a few years and had gotten a stronger idea of who he was and what he desired from life. He no longer needed to conceal or comply, and his friendship with Furnish enabled him to be his genuine self.

The duo rapidly became inseparable, and their relationship evolved into a profound commitment built on similar values, a strong emotional connection, and a love for each other's company.

They complemented each other Furnish supplied a feeling of calm and perspective, while Elton's enthusiasm and inventiveness stimulated and invigorated them both.

In 2005, Elton and David were one of the first couples to join into a civil partnership in the United Kingdom, after the enactment of the Civil Partnership Act. Their choice to legalize their relationship in this manner was not simply a personal commitment but also a public statement in favor of LGBTQ+ rights. Elton had long been a prominent supporter for equality, and by celebrating their union publicly, they helped to strengthen the cause of same-sex partnership recognition, both in the UK and throughout the globe.

Marriage and Public Advocacy

When same-sex marriage was permitted in the UK in 2014, Elton and David were among the first to transform their civil partnership into a formal marriage. Their wedding, conducted in a small, private ceremony, was a beautiful celebration of their love and a sign of how far LGBTQ+ rights had gone. Throughout their partnership, Elton and David have been strong supporters for marriage equality and LGBTQ+ rights, utilizing their position to press for greater acceptance and legal protections for LGBTQ+ persons throughout the globe.

Elton has long talked about how David has been a stabilizing factor in his life, helping him handle the trappings of fame and delivering emotional support during tough moments. Unlike some of Elton's prior marriages, which were impacted by his drug misuse and unpredictable lifestyle, his marriage to David has been defined by stability, openness, and a profound feeling of collaboration. The pair's love and mutual respect have survived for decades, and their public appearances together typically depict a couple at ease with one another and devoted to making a good change in the world.

Becoming Fathers: A New Chapter
For Elton and David, the choice to become parents was a highly personal and emotional move. After several years together, they decided to increase their family via surrogacy. In 2010, their first son, Zachary Jackson Levon Furnish-John, was born, followed by their second son, Elijah Joseph Daniel Furnish-John, in 2013. The advent of their children heralded a new chapter in Elton's life—one that gave tremendous pleasure and contentment.

Fatherhood altered Elton in ways he hadn't imagined. While he had accomplished practically everything a person could hope for in his professional life, being a parent gave him a new sense of purpose and love that surpassed his job successes. He has frequently commented about how his children had offered him pleasure beyond anything he has ever experienced. Zachary and Elijah offered Elton the family he had yearned for—a family founded on love, acceptance, and stability.

Elton has remarked that having children helped him develop a fresh perspective on life. Having spent most of his life in the limelight, with all the expectations and extravagance that celebrity entails, parenthood grounded him in a way nothing else had. His objectives evolved, and he started to arrange his job around his family life. No longer was he willing to be overwhelmed by the pressures of traveling and performing; instead, he concentrated on achieving balance so that he could spend more time with his children and be a present father.

Elton and David have been upfront about the fact that they are raising their boys in an atmosphere where they are encouraged to be themselves and accept their uniqueness. As a couple who have experienced their share of struggles and social pressures, Elton and David are devoted to ensuring that their children grow up in a loving and supportive household where they feel secure and respected for who they are.

Navigating Fame and Parenthood

Being a parent and a worldwide celebrity comes with its obstacles, but Elton has managed to reconcile his family life with his business in a manner that works for him. While he continues to play and travel, he has considerably cut down his responsibilities to ensure that he has time to spend with his boys and David. In interviews, Elton has expressed his thankfulness for the fact that his sobriety and personal development have enabled him to be the sort of parent he wants to be—one who is present, caring, and involved in his children's lives.

Elton's decision to go on his last farewell tour, "Farewell Yellow Brick Road," in 2018 was primarily prompted by his desire to concentrate on his family. He made it obvious that although he would always enjoy performing, his major emphasis was now on being a parent and spending more time with David and their children. The tour, which has lasted many years, has been a difficult farewell to the road for Elton, but he has been open about how delighted he is for the next chapter of his life—one where his family takes center stage.

A Legacy of Love and Family
Elton John's path into marriage and parenting is a monument to his personal development and his dedication to living a genuine and fulfilled life. After years of fighting with his identity, addiction, and the demands of celebrity, Elton discovered stability, love, and happiness in his partnership with David Furnish. Their marriage, founded on a

foundation of respect, trust, and profound passion, has been a source of strength for both of them, enabling Elton to grow both personally and professionally.

As a parent, Elton has accepted his new position with open arms, finding pleasure and significance in raising Zachary and Elijah. His family has given him a feeling of purpose and satisfaction that he had long been yearning for, and his choice to concentrate on his loved ones in the final years of his life represents his willingness to prioritize what matters. Today, Elton John is not only acclaimed as one of the greatest artists of all time but also as a wonderful husband and father who has constructed a life anchored in love, acceptance, and family.

His journey from a closeted, troubled artist to an out homosexual man, loyal spouse, and proud parent is a stunning tale of self-discovery and human transformation. Through his marriage to

David and the pleasure of parenthood, Elton has proved that love, in all its manifestations, is the greatest success of all.

The Later Years – Reinventing the Rocket Man

Elton John's revival in the 1990s and 2000s represented a spectacular second act in his career, re-establishing him as one of the most durable and important artists in contemporary music. After overcoming enormous personal obstacles in the 1980s, including battles with addiction and wrestling with his own identity, Elton emerged from the turbulence with greater clarity and determination. His rehabilitation, both emotionally and professionally, was nothing short of amazing, leading to sustained significance in the music business and a succession of highly lauded productions, most notably his work on "The Lion King" soundtrack.

The Turning Point: Sobriety and Personal Growth

The 1990s were a key time in Elton John's life. After spending most of the 1970s and 1980s fighting addiction, despair, and the trappings of celebrity, Elton chose to stay clean in 1990. This transition offered him a new perspective on life and helped him to reconnect with his music in a deeper, more meaningful manner. Elton has frequently talked about how his sobriety was the key to unlocking a new chapter in his career, enabling him to concentrate on his talent without the distractions that had previously impaired his vision.

One of the earliest hints of Elton's return was the publication of "The One" in 1992, his first album after being clean. The album, which contained songs like the title tune "The One" and "Simple Life," displayed a revived Elton, both musically and emotionally. While his music had always been extremely personal, "The One" was filled with a fresh sense of insight and maturity. The album was a financial triumph, hitting the top 10 in both the UK and the US, and it suggested that Elton was back—stronger and more focused than ever.

The Lion King and a New Audience

One of the most memorable milestones of Elton's rebirth in the 1990s was his work on the music for Disney's "The Lion King". Released in 1994, "The Lion King" became one of the most popular animated pictures of all time, and Elton's contribution to its soundtrack played a vital influence in its success. Collaborating with writer Tim Rice, Elton created numerous songs for the film, including the now-iconic anthems "Circle of Life," "Can You Feel the Love Tonight," and "Hakuna Matata."

Elton's contribution on "The Lion King" was a wonderful match of his musical talent and Rice's lyrical narrative. The songs not only captured the emotional core of the film but also promoted Elton's music to a whole new generation of fans. "Circle of Life," with its strong opening chant and soaring melody, became an anthem that resonated with audiences across the globe.

Meanwhile, "Can You Feel the Love Tonight" received the Academy Award for Best Original Song and the Grammy Award for Best Male Pop Vocal Performance, further solidifying Elton's position in the pantheon of great composers.

"The Lion King" the soundtrack was a major economic success, selling millions of copies and exposing Elton's songs to a younger audience who may not have been acquainted with his prior work. The popularity of the soundtrack also led to the production of *The Lion King* Broadway musical, which opened in 1997 and became one of the most successful and longest-running musicals in history. Elton's music was vital in the musical's success, and his ability to transpose his characteristic sound into a theatrical environment showcased his flexibility as a musician.

Continued Success in the Late 1990s and Early 2000s

Following the triumph of "The Lion King" Elton continued to develop new songs and remain a strong influence in the business. His 1995 album "Made in England" was a return to form, containing the smash song "Believe," which displayed Elton's trademark piano-driven sound and pensive lyrics. The album was well-received by both reviewers and fans, demonstrating that Elton was still capable of crafting songs that connected with a broad audience.

However, the most crucial moment of Elton's rebirth occurred in 1997, when he released "Candle in the Wind 1997," a modified version of his 1973 song originally penned in honor of Marilyn Monroe. The new version of the song was reworked as a memorial to Princess Diana, after her untimely death in a vehicle accident. Elton had been a personal friend of Diana's, and the song encapsulated the worldwide outpouring of sadness that followed her demise. Performed during Diana's burial, "Candle in the Wind 1997" became the fastest-selling track in history and is now one of the best-selling singles of all time.

The triumph of "Candle in the Wind 1997" was bittersweet for Elton, since it was born out of a great personal loss, but it also represented one of the most crucial milestones of his career. The song's worldwide appeal, along with its emotional weight, revealed Elton's extraordinary ability to connect with people on a personal and global level.

Broadway and Beyond: Theatrical Collaborations

Elton's efforts in musical theater didn't end with "The Lion King". His ability to write theatrical music was clear, and he rapidly became one of the most sought-after composers for stage performances. In 2000, he joined up with writer Lee Hall to develop the music for the stage adaption of "Billy Elliot", based on the 2000 British film of the same name. The musical, which depicted the narrative of a little boy who dreams of becoming a ballet dancer, was a critical and economic triumph.

"Billy Elliot the Musical" debuted in London's West End in 2005 and eventually made its way to Broadway, where it won 10 Tony Awards, including Best Musical. Elton's music for "Billy Elliot" was hailed for its emotional depth and ability to convey the essence of the play. The musical's success established Elton's image as a composer who could not only dominate the pop charts but also flourish in the realm of theater.

Continued Relevance in the 2000s

In the 2000s, Elton John continued to create new songs and tour extensively, indicating that his popularity had not diminished with time. His 2001 album "Songs from the West Coast" was recognized as one of his greatest albums in years, with the track "I Want Love," which earned global praise. The album represented a return to the more contemplative, piano-driven style of his earlier work, and it was hailed as a testimony to Elton's continued significance in the music industry.

Throughout the 2000s, Elton remained a busy performer, routinely going on global tours and selling out venues. His live performances, famed for their intensity, showmanship, and spectacular costumes, continued to attract large crowds, and his ability to connect with audiences, both old and new, never decreased. Even when trends in the music business altered, Elton's music remained ageless, and his live concerts became must-see events for fans of all generations.

In 2005, Elton also entered into a civil partnership with his longtime companion, David Furnish, marking a personal milestone that was highly recognized by his fans and the LGBTQ+ community. This connection, and their eventual marriage in 2014, mirrored the shifting views towards same-sex partnerships, and Elton's candor about his personal life further endeared him to fans.

Legacy Projects and Collaborations
As Elton John approached the 2010s, his attention started to move towards securing his legacy. While he continued to create new songs and perform, he also started working with younger artists, teaching a

new generation of musicians and offering his voice to numerous projects. Notably, he collaborated with singers such as Ed Sheeran, Lady Gaga, and Eminem, displaying his ability to accept new musical forms while remaining faithful to his origins.

Elton John's rebirth in the 1990s and 2000s, characterized by his work on "The Lion King" soundtrack and his sustained musical success, was a monument to his persistence, brilliance, and ability to adjust to the times. From his early difficulties with addiction and identity to his personal and professional accomplishments, Elton's narrative is one of reinvention and redemption. His contributions to music, theater, and cinema have left a lasting effect on popular culture, and his ability to stay relevant throughout numerous decades testifies to his exceptional brilliance and influence. Today, Elton John is not only acknowledged as one of the greatest musicians of all time but also as an artist who has consistently pushed boundaries, both musically and personally, throughout his incredible career.

Farewell Yellow Brick Road

Elton John's farewell tour, named "Farewell Yellow Brick Road", marks the conclusion of a major period in music history, putting to a close the live performance career of one of the most influential and adored musicians of all time. The choice to retire from touring was a very personal one for Elton, driven by his desire to prioritize his family and health and to reflect on a legacy that spans over five decades. As the tour progresses, it gives not only a breathtaking celebration of his music but also a poignant meditation on the ongoing effect of his creativity on the globe.

The Farewell Tour: A Grand Finale

In January 2018, Elton John stated that he would embark on a farewell global tour, announcing the end of his live performing career. *Farewell Yellow Brick Road* would run over three years, with more than 300 events scheduled across five continents. The statement caught the music industry by surprise since Elton had been an indefatigable performer throughout his career, renowned for his opulent, high-energy concerts and rigorous traveling schedule.

For Elton, the choice to embark on this farewell tour was prompted by various things. At the age of 71, he had spent more than half a century on the road, presenting thousands of shows to millions of admirers. While his enthusiasm for music and performance remained strong, Elton had come to a stage in his life when other interests, mainly his family, started to take priority. In interviews leading up to the tour, he highlighted that his major motivation for stepping away from live performances was to spend more time with his spouse, David Furnish, and his two boys, Zachary and Elijah. Having spent most of his career absorbed by the demands of celebrity, Elton stated a wish to be there for his children's upbringing in a manner that he had not been able to in the past.

The name of the tour, *Farewell Yellow Brick Road*, was a suitable tribute to one of Elton's most renowned albums, *Goodbye Yellow Brick Road*, released in 1973. The record had long been a fan favorite, and its title tune encapsulated the spirit of Elton's wish for a simpler, more grounded life—themes that now resonated even more powerfully as he prepared to wave goodbye to the road. The farewell tour was planned to be a magnificent retrospective of his career, with lavish stage decorations, film montages, and, of course, his biggest songs. The setlist spanned his vast catalog of music, from early classics like "Your Song" and "Rocket Man" to later hits such as "I'm Still

Standing" and "Candle in the Wind." Each concert on the tour was a journey through Elton's extraordinary career, a celebration of the music that had shaped generations and defined the sound of pop and rock for over 50 years.

A Personal Decision to Retire

While the farewell tour was a celebration of Elton's career, his choice to stop performing was extremely emotional. Elton has always been a workaholic, motivated by an insatiable need to create and perform. Throughout the 1970s and 1980s, he traveled constantly, frequently doing more than 100 gigs a year. The demands of this hard schedule took a toll on his health and personal life, leading to battles with addiction and a feeling of emotional weariness. In the 1990s, after reaching sobriety, Elton continued to travel frequently, but as he neared his 70s, he started to ponder the toll that such a lifestyle placed on him.

Family played a significant influence in Elton's choice to withdraw from touring. Since becoming a parent, Elton had increasingly felt the pull of wanting to spend more time with his children and to be there in their lives as they grew up. While he had accomplished practically everything a musician could dream of—sold-out tours, chart-topping records, and several awards—being a parent gave him a new sense of purpose. Elton frequently commented about how his children had revolutionized his life, giving him a fresh perspective on what was important. He didn't want to lose out on their upbringing, and touring, with its continual demands and time away from home, was no longer compatible with the family life he envisioned.

In addition to family, Elton's health was also a concern in his choice to retire. Years of playing had taken a physical toll, and although he stayed in terrific condition, the rigors of touring grew more onerous as he aged. The lengthy trips, late-night concerts, and continual mobility were no longer as tolerable as they had been in his earlier years. Rather than force himself to continue at the same hectic pace, Elton opted to pull back while he was still at the top of his game, guaranteeing that his last concerts would be delivered with the same fire and passion that had characterized his career.

A Career for the Ages

As *Farewell Yellow Brick Road* went on, it became evident that Elton's decision to retire from touring was not a sign of slowing down artistically, but rather a purposeful choice to shut one chapter of his career while opening another. Even as he prepared to move away from live concerts, Elton continued to work on new songs and collaborations, ensuring that his voice would remain a part of the modern music world. His farewell tour, then, was not an ending, but rather a magnificent climax to one facet of his career—his life on the road.

Throughout the tour, fans and reviewers alike marveled at Elton's tremendous vitality and showmanship. Despite his age, Elton gave performances that were as dynamic and fascinating as those of his earlier years. Dressed in his typical extravagant clothes, with his distinctive spectacles and colorful stage presence, he controlled the stage with the same magnetism that had made him a success in the 1970s. Audiences were treated not merely to a performance, but to an experience—a celebration of a career that had molded the sound of pop music for decades. The tour also had poignant moments, with Elton frequently speaking frankly to the audience about his life, his thanks for their support, and his path through music and stardom.

Reflecting on an Enduring Legacy

As Elton John prepares to retire from performing, his legacy remains firmly intact, with his impact recognized across numerous generations of performers and fans. Few musicians have attained the type of continuous popularity and cultural effect that Elton has accomplished. From his initial recordings in the 1970s to his work on *The Lion King* and his collaborations with modern musicians, Elton has consistently changed, keeping relevant in an industry notorious for its quick swings in trends.

Elton's music, marked by its emotional depth, infectious melodies, and genre-spanning appeal, has touched the lives of millions. His ability to produce classic ballads like "Your Song" and "Tiny Dancer," with thunderous anthems like "Crocodile Rock" and "Saturday Night's Alright for Fighting," proved his flexibility as a lyricist. His association with lyricist Bernie Taupin, one of the longest-running and most successful partnerships in music history, generated a body of work that is unsurpassed in its consistency and brilliance.

Beyond the music, Elton's impact also extends to his daring design choices, his support for LGBTQ+ rights, and his work in charity, notably via the Elton John AIDS Foundation. Throughout his career, Elton has utilized his platform to support issues near to his heart, leveraging his reputation not only for personal achievement but to have a constructive influence on the world. His honesty about his battles with addiction and his path to recovery have also made him a role model for people suffering similar issues, illustrating that it's possible to overcome hardship and continue to create and inspire.

A Farewell, Not Goodbye

While *Farewell Yellow Brick Road* signals the end of Elton John's touring career, it does not indicate the end of his engagement in music. Elton has declared his intention to continue composing and recording new songs, as well as to collaborate on diverse projects in theater and cinema. His passion for music, which has been the driving force of his life, remains undiminished. Even as he moves away from the stage, his impact will continue to define the business, and his songs will be performed and appreciated for centuries to come.

In many respects, Elton's choice to retire from performance is not an ending but a new beginning—an opportunity for him to enjoy the rewards of his effort, spend time with his family, and pursue other creative projects. For fans, the farewell tour is a bittersweet time, as they bid goodbye to the Elton John they've come to know on stage, but it is also an occasion to reflect on the great pleasure and inspiration his music has provided to the globe.

As Elton John takes his last bow, he leaves behind a legacy that is not only measured in records sold or accolades won, but in the many lives he has touched with his music. His goodbye may signal the end of an era, but his songs will live on, ageless and immortal, a monument to the force of music and the genius of Elton John.

Chapter 5

Elton's Creative Process

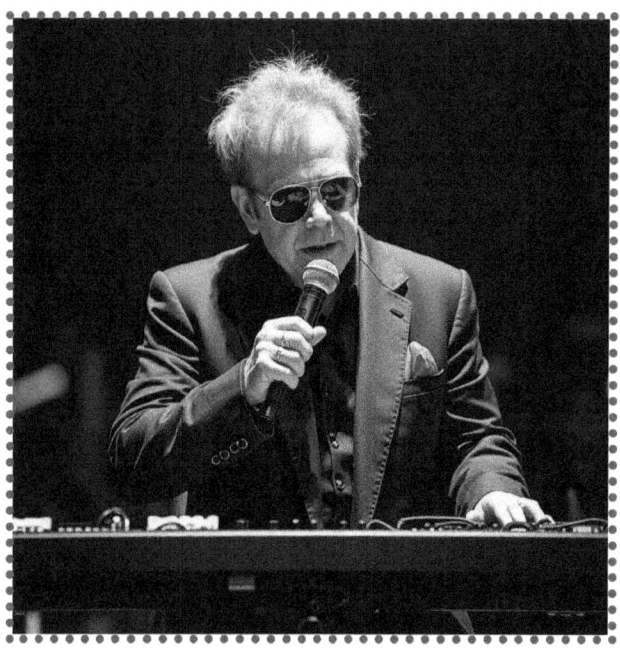

Elton John's approach to songwriting is a monument to his tremendous genius and craftsmanship, marked by a unique combination of musicianship, emotional depth, and a collaborative spirit that has defined his storied career. With over five decades in the business, Elton's songwriting approach has changed, although his passion for making music that connects with people has stayed consistent. His connections, notably with lyricist Bernie Taupin, have been important in molding his body of work, culminating in some of the most adored songs in popular music history. This in-depth look into Elton's songwriting discusses his creative process, partnerships, and the creativity behind his timeless songs.

Elton John's songwriting starts with a great musical sensibility that has characterized his career. He typically defines his technique as one that mixes spontaneous invention with a painstaking attention to detail. Most of his songs start with music, a reflection of his deep-rooted passion for melody. Elton is mainly a pianist, and his composition process often starts at the keyboard. He has commented about how he can sit down at the piano and let the music flow, frequently messing around with various chords and melodies until something hits.

In interviews, Elton has underlined the necessity of being in the correct emotional condition while he writes. He thinks that music should express true sentiments and that the finest songs emerge from a position of sincerity. Whether he is pulling from personal experiences, social challenges, or emotional journeys, Elton seeks to produce music that connects emotionally with audiences. This emotional connection is a feature of his songwriting, enabling listeners to identify the topics and feelings depicted in his songs.

Themes and Influences
Elton John's music reflects a diversity of subjects and ideas derived from both his personal life and

larger societal settings. Many of his songs dive into the complexity of love and relationships, addressing the highs and lows of emotional interactions. For instance, "Your Song," a genuine statement of love, embodies the spirit of vulnerability and honesty, engaging with listeners across generations.

In addition to love songs, Elton's discography explores issues of identity, popularity, and self-reflection. Songs like "I'm Still Standing" and "Sacrifice" reflect his perseverance and contemplation, allowing listeners a window into his journey through the hardships of living in the public glare. His openness to embrace his weaknesses and hardships in his songs has endeared him to followers who see their own experiences mirrored in his work.

Elton's interests vary from classical music to rock & roll, taking inspiration from many genres and performers. He has frequently mentioned inspirations from music luminaries like The Beatles, James Brown, and the operatic masterpieces of classical musicians. This varied combination of inspirations is obvious in his songwriting, as he flawlessly combines many musical genres into his work. The outcome is a distinctive sound that transcends typical genres, appealing to a wide audience.

The Artistry of Performance

The brilliance underlying Elton John's work goes beyond the composing process; it involves his spectacular performances and stage appearance. Elton is recognized for his lavish live presentations, distinguished by bright costumes, complex stage décor, and an infectious enthusiasm that captivates spectators. His performances are a natural extension of his music, bringing another depth of talent that amplifies the emotional impact of his compositions.

Elton's passion for his profession is clear in the way he handles live performances. He typically connects with the audience, providing personal tales and insights into the meaning behind his songs. This connection with his followers converts a performance into an intimate event, establishing a feeling of community among those in attendance. His ability to stir emotions via both his music and his stage persona has made him one of the most famous live performers in history.

Evolution and Adaptation

As music has developed throughout the years, so too has Elton John's songwriting. He has consistently changed his approach to be contemporary while remaining faithful to his creative vision. In the 1990s and 2000s, Elton embraced new musical trends, working with modern musicians and exploring other genres. His desire to experiment with his style, along with his established identity, has enabled him to remain a strong influence in the music business.

Elton's partnerships with contemporary musicians, including Ed Sheeran and Lady Gaga, illustrate his openness to creativity and the merging of generations in music. These relationships not only offer his music to younger listeners but also illustrate his capacity to adapt as an artist. By accepting change while keeping his basic essence, Elton John has proved that real talent knows no borders.

Conclusively, Elton John's approach to songwriting is typified by a beautiful combination of musicianship, emotional depth, and collaborative spirit. His work with Bernie Taupin has created some of the most lasting songs in popular music history, showing the strong interaction between melody and lyrics. Through his music, Elton has explored a diversity of subjects, drawing from personal experiences and larger cultural influences to build a body of work that connects with listeners worldwide.

His genius goes beyond composition, covering his explosive performances and ability to connect with audiences on a personal level. As he continues to innovate and grow, his status as one of the greatest composers and performers of all time remains firmly intact. Elton John's ongoing effect on music and society is a monument to his tremendous genius, and his achievements will continue to inspire generations of artists and fans alike.

The Man Behind the Legend

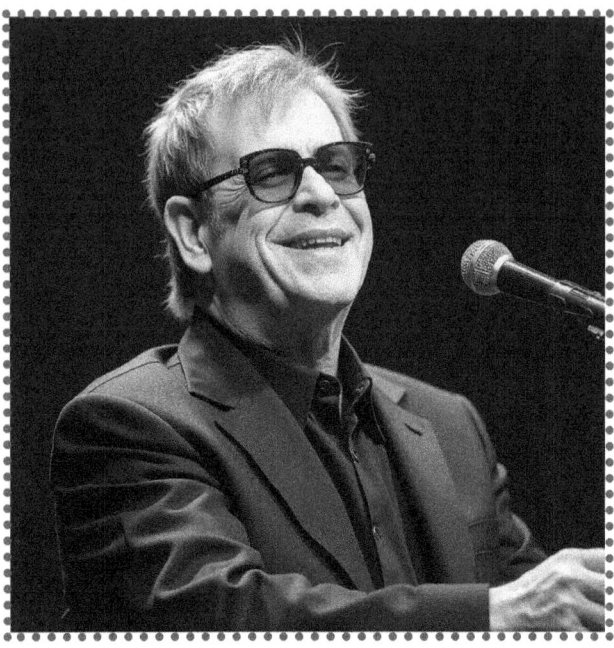

Elton John, beneath the sparkling outfits and renowned performances, is a guy passionately motivated by his passions, vulnerabilities, and a dogged desire to make a difference both in music and in the world. While many remember him as a larger-than-life music sensation, it is the calmer, more contemplative sides of Elton's personality that show his actual intentions and lasting effect.

What Drives Elton Today ?

As Elton John reflects on his life, it's evident that what continues to motivate him is a mix of passion, empathy, and a profound grasp of his weaknesses. In recent years, as he's stepped back from the stage to concentrate on his personal life and his family, he has found new meaning in his duties as a husband to David Furnish and a father to his two children. Fatherhood, he has remarked, has offered him a feeling of contentment and delight that even the brightest spotlight couldn't deliver.

Despite his choice to withdraw from performing, Elton remains strongly committed to music and campaigning. His legacy, both as a musician and as a humanitarian, is far from done. Whether it's via new collaborations, continuous work with his foundation, or just enjoying life with his family, Elton's enthusiasm for making a difference persists.

In the end, the real Elton John is not simply the pop sensation in platform shoes, but a guy who has handled the intricacies of fame, identity, and personal suffering with perseverance and grace. He has utilized his abilities not simply to amuse, but to inspire and elevate, constantly seeking to build a world that is kinder and more compassionate. This is what motivates him and what will continue to define his legacy for centuries to come.

Moral and life lessons learned

Elton John's life narrative is a complex tapestry of achievements, tribulations, and personal development, presenting several moral and life lessons that appeal to audiences across generations. His path from a small-town lad with a love for music to a worldwide sensation and philanthropist is not only remarkable but also delivers great lessons about perseverance, honesty, and the value of giving back. Here are some of the main moral and life lessons that may be gathered from Elton John's story:

1. Embrace Your Authentic Self

One of the most important lessons from Elton John's life is the significance of accepting one's self. Growing up as Reginald Dwight, Elton battled with his identity and felt pressure to conform to society expectations. However, when he matured into Elton John, he completely embraced his identity, including his sexuality and flamboyant lifestyle. This voyage tells us that being honest with oneself is vital for personal happiness and satisfaction. By enjoying who we are, we may encourage others to do the same and create a more inclusive and welcoming society.

2. Overcoming Adversity

Elton John's life is a tribute to the strength of tenacity in the face of hardship. He has endured various hardships, including a rough background, bouts with addiction, and the trappings of stardom. Instead of letting these barriers define him, Elton converted his grief into creativity and utilized his experiences to become stronger. His path indicates that failures may lead to personal development and that overcoming hardship is frequently a critical step toward reaching one's objectives. It inspires people to confront their issues head-on and emerge from them with fresh power and purpose.

3. The Power of Music and Creativity

Elton John's biography shows the transformational power of music and creativity. From an early age, music provided him an avenue for expression and escape from the struggles he encountered. Throughout his career, Elton has utilized his music to connect with people and express profound feelings, proving how art can be a powerful instrument for healing and communication. This lesson stresses the value of following creative hobbies, as they may bring consolation, pleasure, and a sense of purpose in life. It enables people to explore their creativity and discover methods to express themselves genuinely.

4. The Importance of Collaboration

Elton John's successful cooperation with songwriter Bernie Taupin highlights the significance of teamwork in attaining excellence. Their synergy—combining Elton's musical abilities with Bernie's literary genius—has created some of the most memorable songs in music history. This partnership tells us that teamwork may strengthen our strengths and lead to spectacular accomplishments. It reminds us that sharing ideas and working together may result in creativity that is frequently greater than the sum of its parts. By respecting cooperation, we may learn to understand the abilities of others and work toward shared objectives.

5. Addressing Mental Health and Vulnerability
Elton John has been honest about his difficulties with mental health, addiction, and self-doubt. His openness to acknowledge these concerns has helped destigmatize talks about mental health, emphasizing that it is appropriate to seek treatment and be vulnerable. This lesson stresses the significance of mental well-being and urges people to prioritize their mental health. It also serves as a reminder that vulnerability is a strength, enabling us to connect with others and seek help when

required. Elton's experience illustrates that we are not alone in our troubles and that seeking out support is a critical part of the healing process.

6. Giving Back and Making a Difference

Throughout his career, Elton John has utilized his platform to advocate for different causes, notably in the battle against HIV/AIDS and support for LGBTQ+ rights. His charitable efforts via the Elton John AIDS Foundation have generated millions for research and prevention, showing the significance of leveraging one's voice and resources for the greater good. This lesson shows us that we all have the potential to make a difference, no matter how large or little. It inspires people to identify causes they are passionate about and contribute constructively to their communities, reminding us that acts of kindness and advocacy may produce genuine change.

7. The Value of Perseverance

Elton John's route to stardom was not without its challenges, including rejections and losses early in his career. However, his endurance and passion helped him to overcome hurdles and fulfill his ambitions. This lesson shows the significance of keeping devoted to our objectives, especially when confronted with setbacks. It encourages people to create resilience, stay focused on their ambitions, and never give up, no matter how rough the route may appear. Elton's tale serves as a reminder that hard work, commitment, and persistence are frequently vital factors for success.

8. The Significance of Relationships and Support

Elton John's connections with family, friends, and colleagues have played a key part in his life. His relationship with Bernie Taupin, his strong connections with other artists, and his eventual marriage to David Furnish demonstrate the necessity of surrounding oneself with helpful persons. These interactions bring support, inspiration, and a feeling of belonging. This lesson stresses that building meaningful relationships with people is crucial for personal development and pleasure. It encourages us to appreciate our connections and acknowledge the influence they may have on our lives.

9. Legacy and Reflection

As Elton John reaches the end phases of his career, he muses on his legacy and the influence he wishes to leave behind. This contemplation reminds us of the significance of examining the imprints we leave in the world. It encourages people to reflect on how their activities, both great and little, might form their legacy and affect others. By living truthfully, campaigning for issues we believe in, and developing relationships, we may leave a legacy that inspires future generations. Elton's story urges us to review our lives and seek to have a good effect.

Conclusion

Elton John's life narrative is a deep investigation of the human experience, loaded with truths that resonate on both personal and social levels. From embracing honesty and conquering hardship to the value of creativity, teamwork, and giving back, Elton's journey serves as an example for anyone navigating their pathways. His devotion to music and activism illustrates the transformational power of passion and resilience, reminding us that we all have the potential to make a difference in our own lives and the lives of others. Ultimately, Elton John's narrative urges us to live genuinely, chase our passions, and build a legacy that represents our beliefs and aspirations.